BY THE SAME AUTHOR

Poetry

The Sound of Rooms

Night Patrol

Landscaping

Family Plot

Looking for Robert Johnson

Clabber Street Blues

GREEN TOBACCO

GREEN TOBACCO

JOSEPH ALLEN

Greenwich Exchange
London

Acknowledgements

The author wishes to acknowledge the following publications in which some of these poems first appeared: *Agenda*, *Stand*, *Visions*, and the editors of the anthologies *We're All In It Together: Poems for a DisUnited Kingdom* (Grist Books), and *Chasing Shadows* (Culture Ireland).

Greenwich Exchange, London

First published in Great Britain in 2022
All rights reserved

Green Tobacco © Joseph Allen, 2022

This book is sold subject to the conditions that it shall not, by way of trade or otherwise, be lent, resold, hired out or otherwise circulated without the publisher's prior consent in any form of binding or cover other than that in which it is published and without a similar condition including this condition being imposed on the subsequent purchaser.

Printed and bound by imprintdigital.com
Cover design by December Publications
Tel: 07951511275

Greenwich Exchange website: www.greenex.co.uk

Cataloguing in Publication Data is available from the British Library

Cover art: courtesy of Shutterstock

ISBN: 978-1-910996-61-4

CONTENTS

Watching the River Flow *11*
Ham *13*
Girl Singing *14*
Sophie Scholl *15*
Birth of a Revolutionary *16*
The Vienna Woods *17*
Obituaries *18*
Aeolus *19*
Aceldama *20*
Berlin *21*
The Dance *22*
Momento Mori *23*
Ilse Koch *24*
Midi Time *25*
Cellophane *26*
The Potter's Field *27*
The Shortest Verse *28*
Time is Elastic *29*
The Factory Yard *30*
On the Road *31*
Wildwood Flower *32*
Slavic *33*
Out There *34*
Impression *35*
Roll Call *36*
The Hare *37*
Marina del Pisa *38*

Karen *39*

Funeral *40*

The Prisoner *41*

Green Tobacco *42*

Theresa *43*

The Historians *44*

Son House *45*

My Black Pony *47*

Natchez Burning *49*

Huddie *51*

Devil Got My Woman *52*

Footbridge *53*

Faith *54*

Cherry *56*

White Moon *58*

Barrel *59*

Passing *60*

Gas *61*

The Dead *62*

Palestine *63*

Tadzio *64*

Exodus *65*

Together *66*

Distant Days *67*

The Storeroom *68*

The Snow Goose *70*

Kirkinriola *71*

Pointing *72*

Chet *73*

Clouds *74*
Cross-country *75*
Old Bones *76*
Rod 57 *77*
Ishmon *78*

WATCHING THE RIVER FLOW

From my window there is a river view,
a pathway running along its side,
dog walkers, couples, pass by
wrapped against the cold.
I play guitar as I watch,
minutes feel like hours, hours feel like days
and I feel just like Willie Brown
trying to see his future.

This river swallowed my school friend,
spat him out on the bank
across the field from the army officers' houses
and there he lay, peaceful
in the afternoon sun,
waiting to be found.

As holy now as the Ganges
we swam its forbidden currents,
the slow-eyed cattle
watching us from Kernighan's lane,
the weeds as enticing as Ophelia
to our adolescent minds.

We fished for sticklebacks along its shallows
with a father who took us
to where the river bends,
unaware of the tension
between two lovers.

We sketched its eddies,
pencil and pastel merging
like the oil-slicked surface,
I plot its course on maps
drawn by unfamiliar hands,
childish explorers
searching for the source.

HAM

As Gagarin and Titov circled the earth
and Kennedy floundered in the Bay of Pigs
my mother lay in hospital,
'Wooden Heart' and 'Take Five'
sounding from the radio.

Berlin waited for its bisection
and in Ketchum, Hemingway
followed his father's example,
ending his Hemochromatosis with a shotgun,
as my mother watched the nurses
screen her bed from the ward.

And on that Sunday morning,
as Algeria waited for freedom,
Yvor Winters took his Bollingen,
on my brother's second birthday,
I was delivered against the odds,
born laughing like Ham.

GIRL SINGING

I once knew a girl who sang,
looked into the crazy light
and saw life without colour.

The memories of childhood
I held up my collection of faded photographs
to a new generation
who comment without meaning.

Light and shade shape the world,
gives depth to perception,
infancy spent in shadows,
a face held towards the sun,
listening to a girl singing.

SOPHIE SCHOLL

A sunny day Sophie
still you have to go,
yellow star, a Kristallnacht,
twenty-two years is not enough.

You are modern,
a girl I might meet at work
or ask out on a date,
your strength shines,
for all those who were sacrificed.

And I could take a stand
against persecution,
speak out against wrong,
touched with your grace and courage.

BIRTH OF A REVOLUTIONARY

Soso and the Black Spot
were not so different,
Keke birthed them both,
while crazy Beso stitched his boots
and cried for his lost son.

The bloody baptism of Batumi,
as a priest in women's clothing
lost himself in seven rings.

Exile was a badge
worn by the true,
the eagle hovers
waiting for its prey.

Crooked one,
injured arm and broken legs,
lead us to salvation,
let us kiss the unkempt lips
and live our resurrection.

No seminary rules
restrain our power,
the black spot disappears
with the nightly raids.

THE VIENNA WOODS

Through the wards
with the same old refrain,
hearts lost in Heidelberg,
promised treasure, buried with their mamas,
the stink, stink, stink
of an institutional bed.

A bottle of beer please,
non-alcoholic, I go to sleep now,
counting each song of a canary
along a country road.

The old men leave their diapers
in the corridors,
unable to control their bowels
after contraband sausage and pâté.

They are closing the shutters
at the Goldener Bär,
the sun sets on Königssee
and in the forest
the pine cones close.

OBITUARIES

No expectations for the boy
eating cold toast
in the church schoolroom
shirt sleeves buttoned down

a house built on
chairs of frustration
like barricaded towns

days of bored teachers
an education leading to boring jobs

reading the obituaries
of a generation
among examination results

retirements strung out in shopping centres
hospital appointments
and cranberry sandwiches
drowning in a wave
or aimless dog walks
clinging on

AEOLUS

They teach me the sound of TH and F
encourage me to feel
the difference on my tongue
Aeolus's bag of winds
whistling round my head

how long has this toothless mouth
corrected me
envious of learning
suspicious of books

each Sunday evening
we join Circe's pen of pigs
forced to attend the televised worship
of a sacrilegious house

and I worry about unfinished homework
as Speake returns triumphant
and Spartacus sounds *The Onedin Line*
of another endless voyage

ACELDAMA

I am Iouda,
this is my field
fertilised with entrails
and the first noble truth.

Cyborea, take me,
return me to Kerioth,
the infant ignorance
of my destiny.

Before my birth
you dreamt of patricide
yet Simon was safe
from his son.

Caiaphas, you ask too much,
my burden heavier than any price
my clay unworthy of a potter's hands.

BERLIN

He is alone in Berlin
the unemployed sit in the park
waiting out the hours

Mia is at home
the men are provided for
the house respectable

in Alexanderplatz
the night-time arrests are processed
housewives supplementing unemployment cheques

how to live
even the tramps have millions
blame it on the Jews and Communists
bless the butcher for his pound meat

THE DANCE

Each man ploughs his field
when he falls
bury him

the old man
the pregnant girl
side by side
in this dance

the sky is blue
leaves yellow and red
in the park

in the shadow of the wall
we kiss
walking Berlin
the dead sleep

it has come to this
lost in the mass

MOMENTO MORI

My foreign tongue
grates against
newly-learned accents
uniform in conformity

ghosts meet on corners
fear of passing days
lost in shopping malls
coffee shops
neon-lit bookies

like eyes painted
on death portraits
they stare from the past
seeking something lost

ILSE KOCH

Many felt these gloves Margarete
soft like chamois
expensive silk

the riding crop
children serving you
Gnädige Frau

to dispel your boredom
crying in sleep
Jedem das Seine

MIDI TIME

The Midi in the sunlight
through the overhanging trees
the slow movement of boats
in the green water
time slipping in a haze of Bordeaux
as the evening closes in
and a house draws down its shutters
like tired peeling eyes –
I am left with the failing light
to look back at myself
each day passing

CELLOPHANE

Our lives in cellophane
playing out the past
the sash round my grandfather
buses burning in orange flames
a warning at the ferry terminal
to turn back across the water

the concrete barriers
identities checked
then rechecked
Friday night pay packets
littering the streets
around the roadhouse

THE POTTER'S FIELD

In burned-out buildings
the smoking wood of bomb sites
move shoppers along
the market stalls

second-hand books
smelling of mildew
and neglect

avoiding contact
in the embarrassment
of collective guilt

talking of trivia
our backs against
the headline news

like funerals passing
the pain recedes
and we try again

THE SHORTEST VERSE

It's autumn again
night comes early
unexpected death
workers forget
windows and lights
as they rush for home
alone, I blow notes
into the sky
street lamps
one by one
following steps
like the shortest verse,
Jesus wept

TIME IS ELASTIC

I see you
in death

not aware
that time is elastic
we share as one

I know you
as you might have been
joint in memories

passing the hours
in wet afternoons

together
against eternity

THE FACTORY YARD

Sitting at the table
sound of rain
like the radio –

I wish I was older
but life takes time
to learn envy

I smell the work-yard
at dinner
hear the whistle
the conversations

I am late
for the factory
splintered light
from the Victorian windows

makes the afternoon
ephemeral
like life's renewal

ON THE ROAD

Early morning
in the campsite
the stars fade
like smoke
in the solitude

no breakfast
no work
just another day
like hundreds

I owe money
I steal
tinned meat
bread

sleep on the ground
waiting for work
but content anyway

don't need family
don't need home
I live in bus shelters
derelict buildings
learning to be patient

WILDWOOD FLOWER

My dulcimer sings
like a homecoming
the sweet voice
of spruce and rosewood

Hummel, Langeleik
Scheitholt, Épinette des Vosges
harmonising across worlds
like a Swedish Nightingale

a ghostly melody
echoing through mountains
The Song of Solomon

forever drifting West
trying to outrun
a neighbour's axe
seeking Jordan
on a foreign shore

SLAVIC

Through a glass
we speak in tongues
not heard

silence
like wisdom

the Sundays pass
in solace

in limbo
stretching like days

to the sound
of chapel bells
we bath in kitchen sinks

everything wakes
Russian girls with Slavic mouths
smile away the hours

in this town
nothing is forgiven
not even death
nor hunger, nor thirst
as darkness covers the Sycamores

OUT THERE

It could almost be the Mid West
traffic lights change
on empty roads

one-horse towns
in the headlights
are forgotten

Gilberto's sorrow sings
across motorways –
I talk myself dry
keeping you awake

there is a vastness
that is not felt in the daytime
there is a sense of being lost

IMPRESSION

The minutes could be hours
or days
while we watch the sky redden
from tenement steps

then the street lights glow
an impression
we look to the graveyard wall

thoughts scattering
a Pollock
the flow of a Parker solo

everything is abstract
Monk maps my life
harmonising every mistake

ROLL CALL

After roll call
the different coloured meal tickets
were handed out

those who had paid
were called out first
then half-price
free tickets last

at the back of the class we waited
always behind the kids
who were going to grammar school
the children of the doctors
the solicitors, the shop-keepers

we were destined for the factories
or the building sites

everything was beyond us
and yet I saw
the streets illuminated
like a café at night

THE HARE

After two days
my father returned
bottles of Guinness, Babycham
and a dead hare

my mother and aunt
feigned anger
giggled at the fizzing glasses
the hare hanging from his belt

I was too young to care
playing with bottle-tops
for toy soldiers

his beery breath upon my face
bristles rubbing my cheek
smell of nicotine stained fingers
the sound of a tongue
thickened with alcohol

MARINA DEL PISA

The bus station is hot and dusty
people are arriving early

waiting in queue
for the early morning bus
to Marina del Pisa

the pupils from the special school
are pushing forward to be first
like every morning
excited by another day at the coast

on the bus they eat bread and olives
watch pornography
on their mobile phones
giggling into their hands

in the noon heat
there is no shade
from the melting street
from the white blinding sea front

the children from the special school
are tired of sun bathing
are tired of the waves and the boats –
they run across the road
to the amusement arcade

KAREN

Carika
did you find
your voice

in flattened notes

your bed post
shaped like a banjo
neck

Greenwich
forgot you
in their rush for the new

no open tunings
sliding into blue notes

you longed to be
a substitute
trapped in your own future

FUNERAL

The sun is shining on the Boulevard de Ménilmontant
the flowers are arranged
the tables are set
in the Café Lycée Voltaire

for the family
with the smell and air of the grave
the solemn waiters
escort them to wine and bread

the family have carried Paris on their shoulders
the tourists drinking wine
on the Champs-Élysées
the blinding white paths

the river that flows
beneath the arches and bridges
never changing

THE PRISONER

Rudolf is watching
from an isolated tower
the Irish Rangers guarding him
disrupt his morning prayers

seasons pass
Spring, Summer, Autumn
each have their ways
but Winter hardens its grip
unforgiving, resolute

the Unter den Linden is green now
and in the Tiergarten
men meet other men for love

GREEN TOBACCO

How well you covered
your sins Juet
writing from memory
the ship's missing log

bending to the greater good
abandoning your captain
to the ocean

natives trade
but deserve distrust
canoes laden with goods
wives and bows

I sit by the shore
a handful of maize
green tobacco
the sound of night
so unlike home

THERESA

You are dead
my first knowledge
of mortality
the unfamiliar tears
of grown ups
their awkwardness

the coffin displayed
in the best room
drawn curtains
blotting out sunlight

I walk unnoticed
box of pastry
in my hands
unsure of what to do

the daughter takes
me to her mother
the waxy face, unseeing
feel of cold flesh
on my child's lips

in my bed at night
I think of her
on the other side of the wall
surrounded by wood
and candles

THE HISTORIANS

King Billy on the gable wall,
sitting in the back bedroom
breaking Benzedrine inhalers
into coffee cups

bored of drinking cider
on the country roads
trying to get into pubs
and drinking dens

when school finished
we signed on
forced into Government schemes
digging over the same piece of ground
for a pittance

we were expected to fail
pissed-off, we failed
no qualifications
no safe jobs
no prospects –

we write our way through life
reading thoughts
that lie deep and forgotten

we are the transcribers
of the past

SON HOUSE

Could've been a Baptist preacher
but the blues
wouldn't let me be

travelled around this old Delta
seeking souls for the Lord
but the whiskey and women
were my ruin

old Charlie and me
played everywhere we could
from Stovall's
to Rosedale and on

living the easy life
grew up the hard way
trusting no one
keeping an eye
for the next chance

hung up my old guitar
when the gigs dried up
driving buses
for the City Corporation

young white guy
waiting on my porch
calling me Sir
teaching me my songs

playing in universities
making a living from my music
how times change
before the cooling board

MY BLACK PONY

They call me the Indian
I sing the blues
as we stretch out
on the river bank
drinking cheap wine

the factory horn blows
and Pentecost spews
out its workers
half hour of freedom

we have no time
bottles pass the hours –
saddle up my black pony
before the flood

a knife blade
makes the strings
sound human
mournful in the night

on the hour
the trains pass
shaking bedroom windows
sounding lonesome
in the darkness

it's not safe
on the road

at such an hour
we turn our eyes
from headlights
and pray for home

NATCHEZ BURNING

A Tuesday night,
Hezekiah Early and me
were there
glad of a night off
from the bandstand

everyone was at the Rhythm Club
on St Catherine Street
Walter Barnes & His Royal Creolians
always drew a crowd

Ed Frazier had covered the walls
with corrugated tin for warmth
boarded up the windows
against gatecrashers
Spanish Moss decorated the ceiling
petroleum soaked flit

thank God for those fans
circulating some air
cooling the dancers' heat
crowded together

Walter trying to calm the people
getting the band to play 'Marie'
at his last appearance

but flames swept across
the moss-covered ceiling

folk stamped folk
looking for the exit –

they found them piled
one upon the other
asphyxiated, scalded alive
as the fire hoses
hit the metal cladding –

sometimes I feel the guilt
fleeing from the flames
friends calling out to me

HUDDIE

From Fannin Street
to New York City
I became a man

my guitar a way out
picking cotton from sun up
to sun down
was no life for me

in and out
of the penitentiary
for what I did
and didn't do

bummed around with Woody and Cisco
jumping freights
playing in the fruit-picking camps

never expected fame
playing for white folk in Carnegie
recording songs –
sure felt good

DEVIL GOT MY WOMAN

Ran away from home
at fourteen
had enough of school
had enough of rules

travelled with John Lee
Lightin'
the Reverend Davis

living with a bluesman
at sixteen
washing his clothes
cooking his food
cleaning his rooms

didn't mind
didn't mind him touching me up
for lessons
for the real thing –

later on, me and Stefan
hiked the South
playing diners and mission halls
and you know,
the blues gave me soul

FOOTBRIDGE

This was ours –
the footbridge between estates:

a car slowing down
could be danger
always wary

signs were borders
painted kerbstones
the spoken word
could reveal who you were

we worked side by side
yet lived apart
always suspicious

unwilling to take sides
accepting each other
rejecting hatred
we became the target of both sides

FAITH

On the front step
waiting for the mineral man
waiting for my grandfather

old ghost stories
as we walked the country roads
picking blackberries
along the railway
out to the haunted barns of Bluebell Hill –

to me he was as old as Methuselah
and the two-up two-down
with its outside toilet
was his temple

his wife dead
the three daughters kept house
under his biblical laws

the veined cheeks
the eggshell head
covered with feathery down
yet he demanded respect

his carpenter's forearm still strong
with swallow tattoo
yet he would throw balls of bread at us
like a child

and the dying breath
of a life passed by
under the last supper
crying out for faith

CHERRY

Magenta in the summer heat
the Major walks in the garden
watching us warily

as we unpack dustsheets
tins of paint.

We smoke and drink tea
talk about the crazy daughter
sent home from college

before we start climbing
the long sagging ladders
against the gables

and later in the afternoon
smell the burning wood
from the outhouses –

we watch the flames
from the green
and someone points

to an upstairs window
where the daughter
is standing naked

dreaming of fire

her underwear hanging
and blowing gently
from the branches

of the cherry tree.

WHITE MOON

The white moon
above the counter
of Patterson's butcher shop –

thick rashers fell
from the bacon slicer
the smell of pork
filled the air

a tray of trotters
lay cold and white
congealed in fat

blood dropping
from hung meat
and greasy fingers

the white moon floating
on my aunt's face
shining from above

BARREL

Saturday afternoon
I float along
to shouts
from the Show Grounds
past cows
housing estates
with the smell of hawthorns –
my brothers
watching from the bank
throwing stones:
I'm happy in my barrel
but they catch me
beneath the bridge
how far
I might have gone
is not worth thinking about

PASSING

These are the same country roads
we walked as children
behind parents and grandparents

out beyond the cemetery
and the schoolhouse ruins
like watching ourselves
turning back again

will someone meet our ghosts
at the bend of the road
our presence like hot breath
on a summer day

among the hawthorn
the broken gravestones
the black clouds on the horizon
threatening rain at last

these roads stretch beyond ourselves
preserved in the peat
and the slow evolving of the bog lands

GAS

A rainy afternoon
sitting around the kitchen table
we were too young
for the conversation
everything was obscure

the silent nods and winks
the slow shaking of heads
the small pieces of a story

how an uncle's girlfriend
found solace
in the gas oven

my books kept me anchored
to that Sunday morning
to a dull routine
of living and dying

THE DEAD

We are the dead
haunting familiar places
we speak in whispers

like a child laughing
in the hawthorn
causing the rooks to take flight

we touch upon
the summer afternoons
in our dreams

with the smell
of new cut pine
and the silence of early evening
in the locked-up park

like the feel of stone
on the shadows of our skin

as we fall asleep
under the pictures of The Last Supper
and the long departed

PALESTINE

My father's beliefs were selective
he watched *Songs Of Praise*
without fail
swearing at us when our games
became too boisterous
had no time for churches or ministers
didn't like foreigners
told tales of Arabs
lifting their robes
as they shit in the street
turned North Africa into South
simply by rotating the atlas
thought at the end
the Nazis were right
and we should have fought the French
kept plundered bibles
in his bedroom cabinet
the coloured plates
vivid as Palestine

TADZIO

Björn, how did it feel
to be the beautiful boy
forever a Bishonen
paraded at gay parties
to be kissed and petted
a turnkey in Stockholm's
state prison
studying Mahler
at the Adolf Fredriks School –
did you die in Venice
an icon frozen in puberty
to be thrown from a cliff
in Midsommar
your beautiful head
destroyed in a moment?

EXODUS

The Lord led us
out of the Egypt
that was the Cape Colony
onto the promised land
of the Highveld

our Moses was Louis Tregardt
the chosen one
following the pillars of fire

where had Van Rensburg's
trek gone wrong
dead? turned back?

climbing the Drakensberg's
singing of promised pastures
he led the faithful
to an uncertain future

yet Dingaan's name survives
the conquerors are always guilty
it is the living who write the past

TOGETHER

A mass of dead crows
tied together with string
along the roadside

like a van load
of workmen
picked out from their mates –

we become hardened
to suffering
just news

like earth-cracks
like tsunamis

like a politician
dancing in the aisle
of a supermarket

with a Kingsmill loaf
on his head

DISTANT DAYS

I am working in the poor house
chipping away layers of plaster
chipping away generations
of the poor.

There is dry rot
thick as tree roots
creeping from floor to floor
like a judgement.

I take a smoke break
look out of the small window
at the children walking to school
the young men
idling outside the unemployment office

and I see myself again
bowl haircut
in a hand-me-down uniform
on the same street many years before
as I daydream of distant days.

THE STOREROOM

Alone in the storeroom
painting For Sale signs
the hours drag

the path rises
to the school.

Once this was the bedroom
of an old house

through the small window
I look out
upon the convent grounds
at unfamiliar faces

at the Ursuline sisters
cutting flowers
tending the gardens
the graves

at girls in blue
fading into the darkening afternoon.

I think of when I was a child
waiting beyond the gates
for the bus home

separate from the pupils here
by religion

watchful
stealing blooms
from sacred ground.

THE SNOW GOOSE

We are listening to The Snow Goose
in the blue room –

these are the dark days
the slow passing
of afternoons

burning linoleum
cutting out paper soldiers
building cities from old boxes

our aunt hanging washing
in the airing cupboard
the fire burning low

we are the dead
walking empty rooms

KIRKINRIOLA

It is Autumn
I am wire-brushing gates
priming the exposed iron

working in the quiet
of the old cemetery
throwing withered wreaths
on the rubbish heap

reading meaningful inscriptions
that mean nothing now
in the morning sun

I am left on my own
at the gates each day
to repair walls

to eat my sandwiches
with only the blue distant mountains
and the gravediggers
opening another family plot

POINTING

I am pointing one of the towers
up here I can see my house
the heaped backyards
of the council estate –
how small it all looks

the headstones below
like fallen teeth
date to the eighteenth century
holding fast the dead
who once walked here

who walked across town
to the civic park
that was new then
who kissed under the laburnums

on hot afternoons
with the shouts echoing
from the school playgrounds –

she looks across the manmade lake
in her loneliness on the hill
the statue of Armed Science
guarding the tennis courts
and the forgotten generations

CHET

Hi Henry,
how was Oklahoma?
Glendale, California
must have been a surprise

how I would have loved
to play piano
in Mulligan's Quartet

your broken embouchure
developed another style
your horn ripened with age

how did you meet
those paved streets
three storeys down
from an Amsterdam hotel

like a descending scale
from major to minor
a chromatic rundown of steps

CLOUDS

The plane trees
are evenly placed
along the pavement
in front of the Courthouse
and the girls' private school

my uncle pushed his bicycle
past the hotel
painting rags hanging
out of his boiler suit pockets
whistling loudly

the McKing sisters
fell for my melancholy eyes
as they hung out washing
in the whitewashed yard

my grandfather's pigeons
high overhead
the idle men playing pitch and toss
and the clouds kept blowing in
above the park wall

CROSS-COUNTRY

Running round the water tower
where the idlers keep out of sight
and smoke, scrap, look at porn.

Through the broken showers
dirty with rust
trying to hide our bodies.

On freezing afternoons
we try to break the hardened soil
watched by a bored teacher
who is near retirement
who is half-obscured by pipe smoke.

We were there to learn how to bend
to discipline
to get ready for the factories and the building sites
to accept our lot in life
same as our fathers.

OLD BONES

I can see the top of the pines
from my bedroom window

sleep comes and goes
all day in bed
with a fever

the house is quiet
work-day silence
after the weekend

there is a smell of laundry
from downstairs
voices come and go
in my dreams

neighbours gossiping
comforting my aunt,
her side of the family
never made old bones

ROD 57

After two years
I still have the need to tell you the news

let's talk about music
let's talk about art

let's play the roadhouses
one more Saturday night:

did you see us in the front room
touching your forehead
straightening down your beard

and how long did you follow
your own coffin
along the Cushendall Road

curse us for ignoring you
and the car looking out
from the front of the multi-storey car-park
as we walked quietly in line
with its registration, Rod 57

ISHMON

So Ishmon,
how you dreamt of leaving Byram

learning quick
from Rubin and Louis

playing at juke joints
and fish frys
along Mill Street

recording your Saturday Blues
with Papa Charlie McCoy

did becoming a Baptist preacher
ease your Trouble Hearted Blues

lie easy in Willow Park
Canton remembers your words